Little Guides to
Great Lives

ANNE FRANK

LAURENCE KING

Published in 2019
by Laurence King Publishing Ltd
361–373 City Road
London EC1V 1LR
United Kingdom
Tel: +44 20 7841 6900
E-mail: enquiries@laurenceking.com
www.laurenceking.com

Illustrations © 2019 Paola Escobar

Written by Isabel Thomas

A catalogue record for this book is available
from the British Library

ISBN: 978-1-78627-398-7

Commissioning Editor: Chloë Pursey/Leah Willey
Editor: Blanche Craig
Design concept: Charlotte Bolton
Designer: Stuart Dando
Series title designed by Anke Weckmann

Printed in China

Other *Little Guides to Great Lives*:
Marie Curie
Charles Darwin
Amelia Earhart
Frida Kahlo
Leonardo da Vinci
Ferdinand Magellan
Nelson Mandela

Little Guides to
Great Lives

ANNE
FRANK

Written by
Isabel Thomas

Illustrations by
Paola Escobar

Laurence King Publishing

Anne was a <u>Jewish</u> child who dreamed of being an author. In the early 1940s, Anne and her family went into hiding from the <u>Nazis</u>, who were <u>occupying</u> their home city of Amsterdam. The Nazis were trying to wipe out all Jews living in Europe, along with millions of other people, <u>persecuted</u> just because of who they were.

The diary that Anne kept during her years in hiding was discovered and published after World War II. It became one of the world's most famous books, both for Anne's record of the suffering of ordinary Jewish families during the war, and for her courage, hope, and dreams of a better future for everyone.

Anne was born in Frankfurt am Main, one of the largest cities in Germany. Anne's father was a successful businessman, whose family had lived in Frankfurt for hundreds of years.

**Otto Heinrich Frank
(Father)**

Otto was calm, wise, and a natural leader. Anne wanted to grow up to be just like him.

**Edith Holländer
(Mother)**

Edith was humble and distant. She and Anne often fought.

Margot Betty Frank
(Sister)

Margot was three and a half years older than Anne. She was quiet and hardworking.

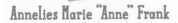

Annelies Marie "Anne" Frank

Anne was lively and chatty. She sometimes got into trouble for speaking her mind.

Like tens of thousands of other families in Frankfurt, the Franks were Jewish.

Anne's early childhood in Germany was comfortable and happy. Her family got on well with their neighbors, and Anne and Margot always had friends to play with.

Anne had no idea that her country was changing around her.

In 1929, the world had plunged into an <u>economic crisis</u> known as the <u>Great Depression</u>, beginning in the USA. This affected everyone in Europe, including Anne's family, who had to move to a smaller, cheaper house.

In Germany, the Nazi Party spread lies, blaming Jewish people and other <u>minorities</u> for the problems that everyone was facing. As Germans became poorer, and more afraid of the future, they began listening to these lies.

I'm scared by the things people are saying. What will the future bring?

The Nazi Party won elections in the early 1930s, and their leader Adolf Hitler became the ruler of Germany. Life for the Franks and other German Jews changed immediately, as the Nazis began taking away the right of Jews to live like everyone else.

Germans were told not to use Jewish businesses, and Jews were banned from government jobs. Jewish teachers were fired, and Jewish children were made to sit apart at school. Anyone who resisted the <u>discrimination</u> was met with violence or arrest. The Nazis took so many prisoners that normal prisons were not big enough. They began setting up prison camps, known as concentration camps, where prisoners were forced to work for free.

Otto and Edith watched in horror as so many of their fellow Germans began behaving in cruel ways towards their Jewish neighbors. Like many Jews, they decided to leave Germany. Otto set up a branch of his business, Opekta, in Amsterdam, the capital city of the Netherlands, and Edith found an apartment there.

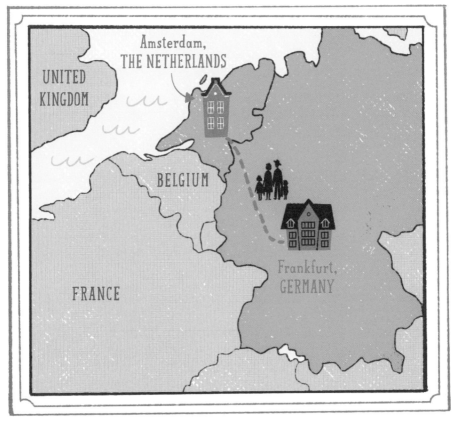

- - - - Route taken by the Frank family

Margot and Anne quickly learned to speak Dutch, and settled in to their new lives. Anne was full of energy and never stopped asking questions. At school, her chatty, cheeky personality helped her to make dozens of friends.

Sanne

Ilse

Hanneli

Anne spent her time just like any other Dutch child —cycling, ice-skating, playing table tennis, looking after her cat, thinking about friendships and fallings-out, visiting ice-cream parlors, and planning what she'd like for her next birthday ...

Just like you, I was excited about the future!

Anne

Jacque

On her thirteenth birthday, Anne was excited to get a diary that she'd spotted while out shopping.

Although Anne was a chatterbox, she found she had plenty to write that she'd never been able to say to anyone in real life.

Anne's first diary entries were about the happy life of a Dutch schoolgirl. But during the Franks' almost nine years in Amsterdam, Nazi Germany had become more powerful.

The Nazis used force to take over neighboring countries. Their invasion of Poland on September 1, 1939 was the beginning of World War II. In May 1940, German troops invaded France, Belgium, Luxembourg, and the Netherlands. In each country they conquered, the Nazis spread hate against Jews and other groups of people.

Soon the discrimination and persecution that the Franks had fled in Germany began in Amsterdam. Jews were banned from government jobs, and Jewish businesses were confiscated. To protect his business, Otto transferred control to his colleagues Victor Kugler and Jo Kleiman, and renamed the company Gies & Co.

Victor Kugler
(Business partner
and accountant)

Johannes "Jo" Kleiman
(Bookkeeper)

Anne had to move to an all-Jewish school. Otto and Edith tried to protect their daughters from worry, while they secretly explored ways to leave the country.

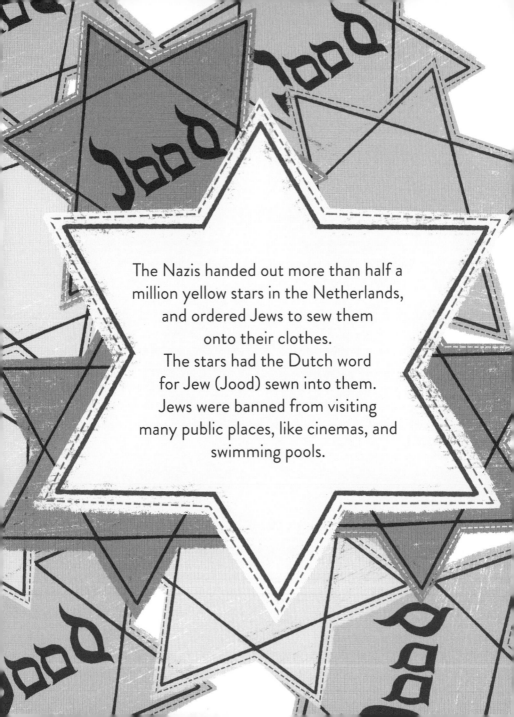

The Nazis handed out more than half a million yellow stars in the Netherlands, and ordered Jews to sew them onto their clothes.
The stars had the Dutch word for Jew (Jood) sewn into them.
Jews were banned from visiting many public places, like cinemas, and swimming pools.

In her diary, Anne wrote about how the country was changing.

These cruel laws were only the start—the Nazis planned to round up and eradicate all Jews in Europe. Many concentration camps had become centers of execution.

On July 5, 1942, a letter arrived demanding that Margot register to be sent to a Nazi work camp in Germany. She was just 16.

Otto and Edith had been planning to go into hiding. They decided it was too dangerous to wait, so they put their plan into action straight away, with the help of Otto's secretary, Miep.

Anne packed the few things that would fit in her school satchel, and said goodbye to her cat, Moortje.

Jews were banned from public transport, so Margot had cycled ahead to the secret hiding place, led by Miep. Anne and her parents set off on foot. Anne was amazed when they arrived at ...

Prinsengracht 263

Gies & Co.

... my father's office?!

Hidden behind Otto's office was a small "back house," which became known as the Secret Annex. Otto had turned it into an apartment where he could hide along with his family, and that of his Jewish business partner Hermann van Pels.

The only other people who knew about the Secret Annex were Jo Kleiman, Victor Kugler, and a few other employees, who Otto trusted like family.

Gies & Co.

"Bep" Voskuijl
(Office clerk)

"Miep" Gies-Santrouschitz
(Otto's secretary)

Jan Gies
(Miep's husband)

Johan Voskuijl (Warehouse manager, father of Bep)

They were willing to help the Franks hide by bringing food, clothes, and company—though helpers risked being sent to prison, or even shot.

Over several weeks, Otto had stocked the Secret Annex with food, clothes, furniture, and bedding. They weren't expecting to go into hiding for another ten days, so everything was piled up in the tiny rooms. At first Anne didn't mind the hiding place. But a week later they were joined by a second family: the van Pels.

Hermann van Pels
A butcher who had joined Otto's business in 1938.

Auguste van Pels
Hermann's wife.
The van Pels had hoped to emigrate to the United States.

In November 1942, the hiding place became even more cramped when the eighth occupant arrived. Fritz Pfeffer was a 54-year-old dentist, who had fled Germany after a night of terrible violence against Jews. He shared a room with Anne, who was not impressed by this fussy, middle-aged man. In her diary she nicknamed him Dussel, meaning "idiot."

Peter van Pels
The only child of Hermann and Auguste. He was 15 when he moved to the Secret Annex.

Fritz Pfeffer
Fritz had been Miep's dentist. He was divorced with a son, who had been sent to England for safety.

The entire Secret Annex was around 500 square feet—smaller than a typical classroom.

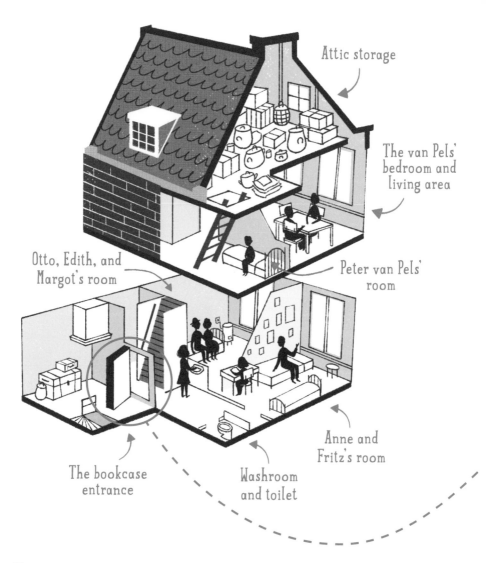

Attic storage

The van Pels' bedroom and living area

Otto, Edith, and Margot's room

Peter van Pels' room

The bookcase entrance

Washroom and toilet

Anne and Fritz's room

Johan Voskuijl built a bookcase across the door to the Secret Annex, so no one using the building would suspect that there was a hidden entrance there.

Life in the Secret Annex was shaped by the need to keep quiet.

Not all the workers in Otto's business knew about the hiding place, so during the working day the eight occupants tiptoed around and talked in whispers. When there were visitors in the office just below the annex, no one could talk, move, or use the toilet at all.

The daily routine for the occupants revolved around not being seen or heard by anyone from outside the Secret Annex:

- 6.45 am   Woken by alarm clock.

- 7.15 am   Get ready before warehouse workers arrive.

- 8.30 am   No one can run water, flush a toilet, talk, or walk around.

- 9.00 am   Office staff arrive. Occupants have breakfast and spend the morning reading, learning, or speaking in whispers.

- 12.30 pm   Warehouse workers go home for lunch. Occupants have a chance to do noisier things, such as vacuuming. Helpers often visit.

- 1.45 pm   Anne uses the quietest part of the day to work and write.

- 5.30 pm   Workers go home for the day. The teenagers could leave the Secret Annex and explore the empty office building. They listened to foreign radio stations and ate dinner.

- 8.45 pm   Bedrooms prepared for sleeping.

- 9.00 pm   Everyone takes turns in the toilet, washing in the sink, and brushing their teeth.

- 10.00 pm   Bedtime.

Anne quickly felt bored and impatient. In her diary, she wrote about the many different ways that the occupants of the Secret Annex passed the long hours.

Picking fleas off the furniture
(from Peter's cat, Mouschi)

Daydreaming

Doing quiet exercises
on the spot

Knitting

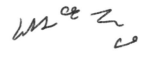

Doing home-education
courses, such as shorthand

Schoolwork
from books

Helping with small jobs
for the company

Telling jokes
and riddles

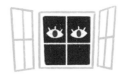

Staring at neighbors
and people on the
street or canal—but
only in the dark!

Trying out new
hairstyles

Practicing different
languages

Miep and Jo borrowed books from the library, and smuggled them into the Secret Annex.

Anne's favorite author was Cissy van Marxveldt, who wrote stories about a headstrong young woman called Joop ter Heul.

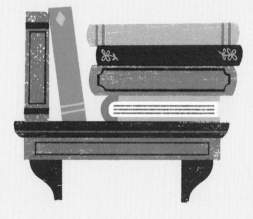

Anne also loved biographies, and Roman and Greek mythology.

A big part of each day was also spent preparing food. The helpers bought <u>ration books</u> on the <u>black market</u>, so they could buy more than their share of food and deliver it to the Secret Annex.

No one knew how long the Franks, the van Pels, and Fritz would be in hiding, so at the start they stocked up on food that was canned or dried. Fresh fruit was turned into jelly, vegetables were preserved, and meat was made into sausages and dried.

For the first few months there were regular deliveries of fresh bread, fruit, and vegetables. Extra rations were even used to bake treats like cakes and cookies. But as time went on, the Nazis arrested some of the suppliers, and their helpers struggled to get hold of enough food for two families. They found themselves eating the same thing for days on end—spinach, potatoes, and boiled lettuce were often on the menu. Even rotten vegetables were a treat.

Writing in her diary was Anne's favorite activity. Inspired by the *Joop ter Heul* books, Anne began writing her diary entries as letters to Kitty, her favorite character.

Although the annex was more crowded than ever after Fritz's arrival, Anne began to feel lonely. The diary became her best friend. She filled the pages with entertaining stories of day-to-day life, as well as her hopes and dreams for the future. Writing also allowed Anne to share strong thoughts and feelings that she did not dare say aloud.

While most days were peaceful, quiet, and dull, nights in the Secret Annex could be noisy.

First there was the

CReeEak!

of beds ...

then the

DONGGGGG!

of the bells of the Westerkek church tower.

Anne was often kept awake by Fritz's

SNOOOOOOORES

... and the

RATTA-TAT-TAT-TAT!

of machine guns aimed at planes flying over Amsterdam.

But worst of all was the

WAAAAAAAAAAAAAAAAH

of the air raid sirens ...

Anne often ran through to sleep in her parents' bed.
Otto comforted her by telling stories that he had
made up for Margot and Anne when they were little.

The mixture of boredom and fear made the mood in the Secret Annex very tense. The families began to bicker. As the youngest and liveliest, Anne often felt picked on. She fought with Margot and her mother. Squabbles between the families also arose, especially between the two mothers.

The atmosphere bothered Anne—she even began dreaming of quarrels—but she used her growing skill as a writer to turn them into funny episodes in her diary.

Anne filled her first diary quickly, and soon began a new one in a notebook. She also wrote short stories, fairy tales, memories, <u>essays</u>, and a novel called *Cady's Life*. From a tiny bedroom hidden from the world, Anne created dozens of new worlds in her mind.

Katrien

Happiness

Fear

Eva's Dream

Blurry the Explorer

Kaatje

Riek

The Flower Girl

A. F.

Cady's Life

The Wise Old Gnome

In March 1944, the occupants of the Secret Annex listened to a radio broadcast by a member of the Dutch government.

We ask the Dutch people to keep any diaries and letters they write during the war, to help the world understand what we have gone through!

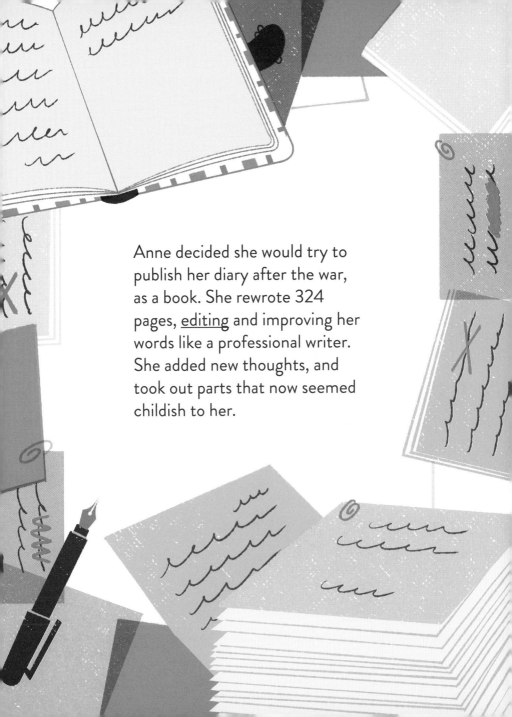

Anne decided she would try to publish her diary after the war, as a book. She rewrote 324 pages, <u>editing</u> and improving her words like a professional writer. She added new thoughts, and took out parts that now seemed childish to her.

The radio sometimes brought moments of joy, including the news of the <u>D-Day landings</u>. On June 6, 1944, <u>Allied forces</u> invaded Europe via five beaches in Normandy, France. This began the long process of freeing France and other occupied countries from German control.

The residents of the Secret Annex hugged and cried as they heard the news. Anne wondered if it was too good to be true, but for a while it brought fresh hope.

But news from outside the house also brought fear.
More and more Jews were being rounded up and sent
to their deaths by the Nazis. Around 25,000 Dutch
Jews had gone into hiding like the Franks, supported
by thousands more helpers.

In May 1944, the grocer who supplied the house with fruit and vegetables was arrested for hiding two Jews. People were offered money for each Jew they betrayed. The residents of the Secret Annex lived in constant fear of betrayal.

Anne's diary shows that her moods swung from joy to misery, and from hope to despair.

She reasoned that they were luckier than many, and was grateful to their helpers. Sometimes just peeking out of the window made her heart soar with happiness.

At other times, Anne was desperate for life to begin again. She longed to go outside, and daydreamed about riding a bike, breathing fresh air, seeing her friends, and returning to school.

Anne's diary entry of August 1, 1944 was the last she ever wrote.

On the morning of August 4, 1944, members of the Dutch police and <u>Gestapo</u> entered Prinsengracht 263 with guns, and demanded to search the building.

Otto, Edith, Margot, Anne, Auguste, Hermann, Peter, and Fritz were discovered, arrested, and taken away in a truck.

No one knows if the occupants of the Secret Annex were betrayed, or if it was a routine search. Two of their helpers, Jo and Victor, were also arrested.

First they were taken to Westerbork, a camp in the Netherlands. On September 3, 1944, they were ordered to board another train. It was the last train ever to leave the Netherlands for Auschwitz, a large concentration camp in Nazi-occupied Poland.

The train reached Auschwitz on September 5, 1944. Around half of the 1,019 people on board were immediately sent to their deaths. The eight from the Secret Annex survived, but the males and females were split up.

Anne, Edith, and Margot were forced
to work 12 hours a day, fed barely
anything, and made to sleep in
crowded bunks.

In late October or early November
1944, Anne and Margot were
moved again—this time to the
Bergen-Belsen concentration
camp in Germany. Edith remained
in Auschwitz, where she died in
January 1945.

At Bergen-Belsen Anne and Margot
were still together, but starving and
weak. Illnesses spread quickly in the
terrible conditions. The sisters caught
<u>typhus</u> and died in February or
March 1945. Anne was 15.

Just a few months later, in May 1945, Germany surrendered and the war in Europe finally ended. Survivors in the concentration camps were freed. Six million Jews had died during the <u>Holocaust</u>, along with five million other people murdered for who they were. Of the residents of the Secret Annex, only Otto Frank had survived.

Otto arrived back in the Netherlands in June 1945. He hoped to find Margot and Anne, but when he spoke to a Dutch woman who had been in Bergen-Belsen he discovered that they had died.

Miep had rescued Anne's diary and papers from the Secret Annex. She gave them to Otto, who was amazed to read about Anne's inner thoughts, and her plans to become a writer.

Otto devoted the rest of his own life to sharing Anne's story with the world.

Het Achterhuis (The Secret Annex) was published on June 25, 1947.

More than 70 years later, Anne's diary has been read by millions of people around the world, from world leaders to school children. It has been translated into more than 70 languages, as well as being made into films, plays, and TV programs.

Anne's diary has helped generations of people to understand the impact of war on human beings. It reminds us that the things we have in common are far more important than what makes us different.

Read Anne's diary and let her inspire you to make the world a better place!

TIMELINE

June 12, 1929
Anne is born in Frankfurt am Main, in Germany.

October 1929
The Great Depression begins in the USA and spreads across the world. Anne's family are forced to move to a more modest home.

Early 1930s
The Nazi Party comes to power, and life for Jews in Germany becomes difficult. The Franks decide to move to Amsterdam when Anne is four years old.

June 12, 1942
Anne receives a diary for her thirteenth birthday and writes her very first entry that day.

July 5, 1942
A letter arrives, saying that Margot is to be sent to a Nazi work camp back in Germany.

July 5–6, 1942
Fearing for their lives, the Franks go into hiding. They move into the Secret Annex behind the offices at Prinsengracht 263.

June 1944
The inhabitants of the Secret Annex hear news of the D-Day landings on the radio.

August 1, 1944
Anne writes her last diary entry.

August 4, 1944
The eight inhabitants of the Secret Annex are discovered and sent to Westerbork camp.

May 1945
The war ends in Europe.

June 1945
Otto returns to the Netherlands, where he learns that he is the family's sole survivor. Miep has kept Anne's diary safe during the war, and she gives it to Otto.

June 1947
Otto arranges the publication of Anne's diary as *The Secret Annex*.

September 1939

World War II breaks out after the Nazis invade Poland.

May 1940

The Nazis invade the Netherlands, as well as France, Belgium, and Luxembourg.

May 1942

More than half a million Jews in the Netherlands are given yellow stars by the Nazis, and forced to wear them in public.

July 13, 1942

The Franks are joined in the Secret Annex by the van Pels family.

November 16, 1942

Fritz Pfeffer moves into the Secret Annex, where he shares a bedroom with Anne.

March 1944

Anne hears a radio broadcast asking the Dutch to keep their diaries as records of wartime, and starts editing her diary.

September 3, 1944

All eight are transferred to Auschwitz, but here the males and females are separated.

October/November 1944

Anne and Margot are moved to the Bergen-Belsen concentration camp.

February/March 1945

Both Anne and Margot die from typhus.

Today

Anne's diary has been translated into more than 70 languages and read by millions.

Anne Frank

Otto Frank founded the Anne Frank Fonds in 1963, and it continues to ensure Anne's diary is always available in print, and reaches as many people as possible. The proceeds are used for charity and education.

GLOSSARY

Allied forces—the countries that fought against Germany, Italy, and Japan in World War II.

black market—things that are sold on the "black market" are not sold in stores, but secretly, unseen by the authorities.

D-Day landings—an event that took place on June 6, 1944, when the Allied forces arrived by sea and landed on beaches in Normandy, ready to drive the Nazis out of France.

discrimination—treating people unfairly because they are thought to be different.

economic crisis—a time of financial struggle, when prices become very low, banks collapse, and many people struggle to find a job.

editing—making changes or improvements to a piece of written work.

essays—pieces of writing in which an author gives their opinions on a chosen subject.

Gestapo—the German secret police under the Nazis. The Gestapo was responsible for controlling the activities of Jews, and for transporting them to concentration camps.

Great Depression—an economic crisis that began in the USA in 1929 and spread around the world. It lasted for several years.

Holocaust—the name given to the murder of six million Jews by the Nazis during World War II.

Jewish—Jewish people are followers of the ancient religion known as Judaism. People from Jewish families are often still called Jewish, even if they don't follow the religion anymore.

minorities—smaller groups of people who are considered different to the rest of society, often because of their race or their religion.

Nazis—supporters or members of the Nazi Party, or the National Socialist German Workers' Party, led by Adolf Hitler, which took control of Germany in the 1930s and led it into World War II. After the war the Nazi Party was declared illegal.

occupying—when the government of one country takes control of another country. The Nazis occupied many countries, including the Netherlands, until the end of World War II.

persecuted—when a person or group of people are treated poorly, often because they follow another religion to those around them.

ration books—because food was in short supply during World War II, governments wanted to make sure that everyone received the same small amount. All families were given a ration book, containing tokens that could be exchanged for food, to keep a strict limit on what they bought.

typhus—a very serious disease carried by lice.

FURTHER READING

Het Achterhuis (The Secret Annex) [first edition] (Contact Publishing, Amsterdam, 1947)

Anne Frank: The Diary of a Young Girl, [the definitive edition] (Penguin Books Ltd, London, 2007)

Anne Frank: The Diary of a Young Girl [abridged edition for young readers] (Penguin Books Ltd, London, 2015)

INDEX